Copyright Page

Nubian Dynasty R.O.A.R. Restore Original African Royalty by Kline Jr. Green, Kadin Green, & Janael Palmer

© 2021 by Janael Palmer

ISBN: 978-1-7357977-5-5

Published & Edited by: Simene' Walden, The Student Teacher

P.O. Box 813 Savage, MD 20763

First Printing, January 2021

Printed in the United States of America

All rights reserved. Copyright under Berne Copyright Convention, Universal Copyright Convention, and Pan-American Copyright Convention. No part of this book may be reproduced, stored in a retrieval system, or transmitted in any form, or by any means, electronic, mechanical, photocopying, recording or otherwise, without prior permission of the author.

For permission contact:
info@nubiandynastyroar.com

Dedication

This book is dedicated to my father, Michael Augustine Palmer, who passed away on September 16, 2020.

AFRICA MAP

Africa: It All Began In Our Motherland

The black race originated from Africa.

Africa is surrounded by several large bodies of water.

It is the second largest continent that has 54 beautiful countries.

There were many Africans who were displaced from Africa thousands of years ago who have now adapted to the country they found themselves living in.

These animals are native to the Motherland: Africa. Which animals do you recognize?

The Lies That Portray Africa

The lies and tactics of distractions about Africa are used to turn our backs on the Motherland Africa.

We were the first people and race who started human civilizations and gave birth to all other nations.

Now that we know who we are, we have to reclaim our crowns.

We are a royal people who come from the ancestors and bloodline of Nubian Dynasties of honorable kings and queens.

Restore and Rebuild Africa Within Us

In Restoring Original African Royalty, we have to rebuild and reprogram the black race.

In order to rebuild and restore the original African royalty, we must focus on our black roots.

The Black Queen is the mother and producer of many nations.

The Black Queen is the only woman known to carry the "Eve Gene", which allows her to birth all ethnicities.

We must focus on our black history, black spirituality, the black man, the black woman, the black boy, the black girl, and the black family.

We have to rebuild our practices and our lifestyles to regain our power and get back to our positive ways of life.

Learning and relearning how to Restore Original African Royalty will allow us to change the world with confidence and pride in knowing that our great, great ancestors before the Atlantic Slavery Trade and Colonization, were and still remain the richest, most royal, humble spirited, and powerful creations that ever walked this earth.

Rebuild Black Roots

Black roots are the foundation of where we originate and our unique make up of where we come from.

The roots of the black race is one that is planted in royal descendants.

Africa is our home land and it's our safe place.

As we research the history of the continent and its countries, it will allow us to understand where we come from and also help us understand ourselves better.

We will be exposed to customs and traditions that will no longer leave us lost, but will lead to us discovering who we are.

Seek truth, righteousness, and our roots, in order to receive the peace and wholeness we need about who we are.

Rebuild Black History

Black history is a celebration of our existence.

Black history is a celebration of where we come from, who we are, our contributions to this world so far, and where we are going.

Black history is celebrated during the shortest month of the year.

We must learn our true history starting from Africa and not the British history that has been taught and written about Africa.

African Flags

 Burundi	 Cameroon	 Cape Verde	 Central African Republic
 Djibouti	 Egypt	 Equatorial Guinea	 Eritrea
 Guinea-Bissau	 Kenya	 Lesotho	 Liberia
 Mauritius	 Morocco	 Muzambique	 Namibia
 Seychelles	 Sierra Leone	 Somalia	 South Africa
 Tunisia	 Uganda	 Zambia	 Zimbabwe

Learning our history will allow us to challenge all the odds that have been set up against us to fail.

Africans in America and Africans on every continent must forgive each other and refuse to be at odds with one another.

We are each other's allies.

Black Pride

Black pride is ownership of who we are in our everyday lives.

Black pride is ownership of where we come from.

Black pride is being proud descendants of Africa.

Black pride started when we began to value ourselves.

Black pride includes us affirming who we are everyday.

Rebuild Black Spirituality

Black spirituality is universal human experiences with the world around us that conncets us to The Creator and a deeper meaning to life.

Connecting to a higher power means that we are taking responsibility and accountability for the way we are living.

Connecting to a higher power means we are caring for the things that we have been entrusted with.

Rebuild Black Culture

Black culture embodies our achievements, our qualities, our skills, and our talents that are admired by many.

Our African and African American culture is richly reflected and expressed through our music, our dance, our language, our dress, our foods, our arts and crafts, our folklore, and our spirituality.

As a people, we are very diverse.

Rebuild the Black King

The Black King is the original man and father of civilization.

He is the closest person to God in the human form.

He is the first teacher and educator of knowledge.

He has a strong, masculine physique.

He comes in many variations of chocolate accentuated with dark mysterious eyes, full lips, deep strong jaw bones, and broad shoulders.

Rebuild the Black Queen

The Black Queen is the mother and producer of many nations.

The Black Queen is a Nubian goddess, created in love, strength, resilience, softness, wisdom, and everything pure.

The Black Queen comes in beautiful variations of gorgeous melanin skin tones.

The Black Queen is like a superhero.

♥ Stages of Love ♥

Rebuild Black Love

Black love is a powerful and beautiful bond between a melanin King and Queen.

This love is one that is pure, genuine, and healthy and creates the opportunity for the love birds to bring out the best in each other.

The King leads in love, protecting his queen always, and handling her heart with lots of care.

The queen respects and honors the greatness in her king and speaks life into him to move him closer and closer to his greatness.

Rebuild the Nuclear Black Family

It is true that family is whomever you consider them to be.

The strength of the black family is the responsibility of our black Kings and Queens.

Kings and Queens must be able to put their differences aside to work in a partnership and team to always put forth the best interest of the family first.

The Black King must stand strong as the head of the household.

The Black King must be the provider, protector, and disciplinary of the family that comes from a place of love and best interest of the family.

The Black Queen is the backbone, supporter, and nurturer of her family.

The Black Queen provides love and encouragement to her family.

Rebuild Black Parenting

Black parenting is rearing and nurturing young kings and queens.

Parenting is not an easy job and there is not any right or wrong way to do it.

There are a lot of trials and errors that go into being a parent.

Parents have to be willing to make logical and healthy decisions on behalf of their children.

Parents must have the understanding that being a parent is a privilege and not a right.

It is the responsibility of parents to equip their children for life.

Parenting is about leading by example with their actions and not just telling their children what to do.

Rebuild the Black Village and Community

The black village and community consist of other melanin kings and queens working together to support each other to achieve common goals to strengthen their neighborhoods.

The community holds each other accountable to come together.

The community pitches in helping to raise the upcoming generation of young kings and queens.

The village gathers frequently in fellowship in times of need, to celebrate together, to educate one another, and to help each other to succeed.

Rebuild Black Brotherhood

Black brotherhood strengthens our black kings and challenges us to be accountable to ourselves, our families, and our purpose.

Black brotherhoods have to be the ones to protect their women and children, police their own neighborhoods, put the guns down, look out for each other, and support one another through life's challenges.

The black brotherhood must form or become actively involved in organizations that aid in mentoring and guiding the younger generations of kings that look up to them.

Restore Black Sisterhood

Black sisterhood is a bond and universal code between strong black queens that are formed on an understanding of mutual respect for the struggles of a black woman.

Having a black sisterhood allows one to have a safe space to feel understood and hash out their challenges without negativity, criticism, competition, jealousy, gossip, or any other negative vibes.

The black sisterhood must continue fostering relationships that encourage positive collaborations that promote and display encouragement, support, uplifting, growing together, and leaning on each other.

Restore Black Education

Black education is the knowledge and awareness that will be one of the keys in the success of the black family.

Being educated and seeking to be educated are the beginning steps to free oneself from mental slavery.

Learning and gaining knowledge comes in many forms.

Learning is taking the initiative to gain knowledge every day.

Access to technology allows people to be creative in expressing themselves.

It is also important that black people are taught things outside of a classroom.

The structure needed for learning will allow one to become well rounded individuals who can take charge of our money, our time, our minds to critically think, and how to start and manage a business.

Rebuild Black Ownership, Wealth and Entrepreneurship

The black family must work smart by creating plans and systems that will have their money work for them and generate long term generational wealth.

The black family must create more assets than liabilities.

The black family must start taking interest in investing.

The black family must start taking interest in home ownership, land purchases, and wealth building.

Discuss with your families other areas the black race needs to be restored in order to build these generations back up to be a more united force of power, displaying group love, self-love, and empowerment.

Apply and practice these principles to your life daily.

Engrave and adopt them young so they will become second nature for you.

Meet The Authors
Janael Palmer

Janael Palmer, was born in Freetown, Sierra Leone, which is located in West Africa on October 2, 1986 to Michael and Jane Palmer. Janael's name is pronounced Jah'nel and is a combination of both of her parent's names, that was made up by her late father. She came to the States at the age of six years old to join her parents.

Janael graduated from Coppin State University in 2010 with a Bachelor's Degree in Psychology. She graduated in May of 2012 as a Adult Gerontology Registered Nurse from Howard University. Janael graduated from Maryville University in August of 2018 with a Master's Degree in Adult Gerontology. Janael is the mother of two amazing boys, an author, and entrepreneur.

Kline Jr. and Kadin Green

Kline Jr. and Kadin Green are brothers whose parents are Kline Green Sr. and Janael Palmer.

These two young little men are so full of life, have lots of vibrant energy, and huge personalities to share with the world. They enjoy playing video games, being adventurous, exploring the world, playing outdoors, and socializing with others.

They are athletic boys that absolutely love the outdoors. Kadin Jr. has already had an exciting experience in the social media world that allowed him to go viral on a number of social media platforms. He has been featured on shows like Inside Edition and on one of CBS's At Home Segments.

Nubian Dynasty:
Restore Original African Royalty

Nubian Dynasty Next Steps

3 Ways You Have Been Educated

....

....

....

3 Ways You Have Been Empowered

....

....

....

3 Ways You Have Been Elevated

....

....

....

3 Ways You Will Educate Others

....

....

....

3 Ways You Will Empower Others

....

....

....

3 Ways You Will Elevate Others

....

....

....

After you have read the book, please post a picture and a review of the book on social media. Tag me in your social media post @janaelpalmer. If you do not want to use social media, you can also email all testimonies to info@nubiandynastyroar.com. You have the option to just post directly to Amazon.com as well.

Once you have completed your next steps, please share that with me too. We want to support you on this journey. You can either post to your social media and tag me or email us your next steps.

www.ingramcontent.com/pod-product-compliance
Lightning Source LLC
Chambersburg PA
CBHW051258110526
44589CB00025B/2874